"One cannot look at a Judy Gilder painting without feeling a sense of elati
drama. Her work has a vibrancy that creates a marvelous sense of energy a...
Judy has been a hard-working and enthusiastic participant in my watercolor classes
for years at Santa Barbara City College. Through the diligent practice of acquired
knowledge, skills, techniques, and the exhilaration of 'splashing' watercolor, Judy
has become a superlative artist. Noticeable in her work is her supreme and dramatic
balance of color and temperature. She further supports her paintings with strong
design, creating a directed center of interest by specifically utilizing the elements of
color, shape and texture. Judy is an extremely brave painter, eager to take risks and
embrace new ways to enhance her work. This is not an easy thing for an artist to do,
for many times you create 'a less than beautiful painting' as a result. In the long run,
risk brings change, growth and maturity in an emerging artist. It is with extreme joy
that I have watched Judy develop to become the spirited artist she is today."

Cathy Quiel, Artist / Art Teacher

"Judy Gilder's book takes the reader on a gripping soulful journey from the first page
on. Her story speaks passion with every nuance in heartfelt words and beautiful art.
What would stop most of us cold in our tracks inspired Judy to write, to paint, to
live through her wonderful book what most of us dare not dream of. *From Where I
Sit* is a heroic achievement." Paulette Mahurin, Nurse Practitioner / Author

"I have known Judy Gilder since 1996, and helped record her early writing. Her book,
From Where I Sit, emotionally moves me with its heartfelt essays and marvelous
paintings. I expect it to be wildly successful as Judy shares an important message for
us all." Fred Barton, Mdiv, MA

"As an artist with a disability myself, I'm always inspired by people with limitations
who enjoy expressing their gifts and talents—and fellow artist Judy Gilder beautifully
paints not in spite of her physical challenges, but through them. In her book,
From Where I Sit, the reader will be captivated by her whimsical compositions that
highlight impossibly stunning colors in subtle tones and delicate shades. Although
this remarkable artist displays incredible strength in her brushwork, it's Judy's story
that will grip you the most. I highly recommend *From Where I Sit* to anyone who
is seeking refreshment for their soul, and inspiration for their heart!"

Joni Eareckson Tada, Joni and Friends
International Disability Center

from where I sit

ESSAYS | ART BY JUDY ANN GILDER

EDITED BY MARGARET KAY DODD

BLUE PALM PRESS
Santa Barbara

Serenity, watercolor on paper

Published by Blue Palm Press
P O Box 61255, Santa Barbara
California 93160, USA

Designed by Margaret Kay Dodd, Studio K Arts
studiokarts@earthlink.net

Printed in the USA

ISBN 978-0-9771866-4-8

Frontispiece photo: Judy with Rodin's "The Thinker,"
Santa Barbara Museum of Art, 1995
Title page photo: Judy at Hendry's Beach, Santa Barbara, 1995

dedication

I hope that everything I have to say will help everyone who reads this in some way. I want to be a good influence on people of all kinds, not just people like me. I want all my readers to take what I have to say to heart, with understanding.

To Carol Baizer; Fred Barton; Maria Batres; Lori Boehm; David Briggs; Mario Cervantes; Shella Comin–DuMong; Stephen Day; Jenny Doelling; Erin Doyle; Linda Egar; Elizabeth Flanagan; Lois Gadsby; Christine Groppe; Shirley Hayes; Cathy and Julie Head; Wanda Harrison; Marty Kinrose; Gerard D. C. Kuiken; Rod Lathim; Mark and Asha Lee; Jacob Lesner–Buxton; Petra Lowen; Paulette and Terry Mahurin; Debra Mullin; Kim Olsen; Marty Omoto; Elisa Panizzon; Barbara Parmet; Maria Rocha; Bernie and Ruth Schaeffer; Mary Sharpe; Valerie Simpson; Gene and Tom Smith.

To my friends in Sausalito: Richard Aspen, Matey and Chinook; Jim Collison; John Rogers Dunlop; Carla Reineri.

To my art teachers: Rose Margaret Braiden; Joe Gillick; Cathy Quiel; Kaaren Robertson; Cathy Runkle; Jill Sattler; and to all the students in my art classes.

To my whole family: my parents Isabel and David Gilder; my brother Mark Gilder, his wife Judy; Brian and Lisa Gilder and their children, Lauren and Ryan; David and Jennifer Fishman and their children, Jacob, Ian and Matthew; my sister Elaine, her husband Stephen Jacobs, and their children, Ellysa, Ana and Adam.

To all participants in the Judy Gilder Independent Living Support Group.

To my staff where I live, and to the agencies United Cerebral Palsy (UCP); TriCounties Regional Center; Hillside House; Chance Housing; The Independent Living Resource Center; and the CITY Program in Santa Barbara, California.

To whoever else helped me that I may have forgotten, and to anyone who worked with me to make me a better person.

Especially to Pauline Paulin, who recorded my writing and was always there for me; Elizabeth Anne Howorth, who helped me settle into my new home and remains my friend; Judy Nason, my teacher and long–time advocate, who selected my art and cards for display and encouraged me so often; and Margaret Kay Dodd, who was with me every step of the way in getting my own place, and who edited and compiled my writing and designed the book.

With love,

Judy Gilder

Ann Seeker is my pen name. My first writings were done using this name.

Note: From the time I met Judy, she constantly sought for a word to describe her situation that was not derogatory or that implied separation. "Special" and "handicapped" were words to avoid because they created a stereotype. She preferred the word "disabled" and settled on "rolling people" in the end. And "walking people" to state the difference.   *MKD*

a note

This book, both as art catalogue and memoir, has long been in the making. Beginning at a time when Judy was living in an institution in Santa Barbara, California, her writing was fueled by her emotional states and sense of despair, wanting to live in the outer environment and frustrated by the seeming impossibility of that dream.

Finding an outlet to communicate her frustration led to years of self-expression. Her writing from the early 1990s on explores the innermost desires and feelings of a determined woman of middle years from her unique perspective on her situation. The reader will find much anguish described about what it is like to live long term in an institution. This is Judy's necessary venting. She could not change her situation, but she could write about it.

In 1996, she found another avenue of expression in painting. Both writing and painting soothed and engaged her, helped her live with her circumstances. But once the opportunity came to move away from institutional living in 2003, her priorities changed. Her writing almost stopped altogether, and her paintings took off in new directions.

There were many adjustments to be absorbed after Judy moved to her own home. It took time, and there was no longer the urgency to write after the desperation of her unchanging situation in the institution was over. She devoted herself to settling into her new environment and lifestyle, and her remarkable artwork is testament to her relief and sense of relative freedom.

Though no living is without challenges, Judy, now in her late seventies, can look back at her achievements with some satisfaction. Her voice, expressed through her paintings, rings of a craving for beauty forged from the crucible of intense longing, continuous dedication, and a deep love for life.

Margaret Kay Dodd

Fire and Ice, watercolor on paper

Meeting of the Judy Gilder Independent Living Support Group, 2001. From left: Erin Doyle, Judy Gilder, Margaret Kay Dodd, and Pauline Paulin. Photograph by John Rogers Dunlop

preface

Lessons Judy taught me: Ask for help, never give up—ask for help, gratitude—ask for help, humility—ask for help, determination—ask for help, laughter in abundance.

I first met Judy at the facility where she lived. She was sitting in a corridor with other residents in wheelchairs. I introduced myself as "Anne, your Independent Living counselor." She squealed with excitement, her whole face lit up. I had never had a reception from anyone quite like that before.

The second time we met, I found Judy sitting alone naked in a shower chair in a large tiled bathroom. I covered her with a towel and announced I had been sent to observe her taking a shower and asked her, "What do you think about that?" We both burst into fits of laughter, and I knew from then on, we were on the same page.

Judy is an inspiration to all who meet her. Her courage and perseverance are awe-inspiring. Given her physical disabilities, Judy has accomplished more in her lifetime than many people with perfectly functioning bodies.

I feel privileged to know Judy. She swells my heart.

Elizabeth Anne Howorth

Judy has been my friend for over 30 years. I met her while working with a former writing student of mine at the facility where they both lived. Judy was part of the "greeting" committee: she loved to spend time in the entryway, where all the action was! When my student moved into independent living, Judy asked if I would help with writing a book about her life. I couldn't say no—Judy is very persuasive.

I was moved by her curiosity, her eagerness to be part of things, and her sheer determination to be everything she could be. She wrote often of her desire to live independently in a place of her own. Thanks to her perseverance, knack for getting people together, and the help of her support group, she finally achieved her dream. It is a pleasure to see another dream come true, this book with the writings she started so long ago, together with selections from her paintings.

I call her courageous, but she says, "What else could I do? I just want to live my life the best that I can."

Pauline Paulin

White Series No. 7, watercolor on paper

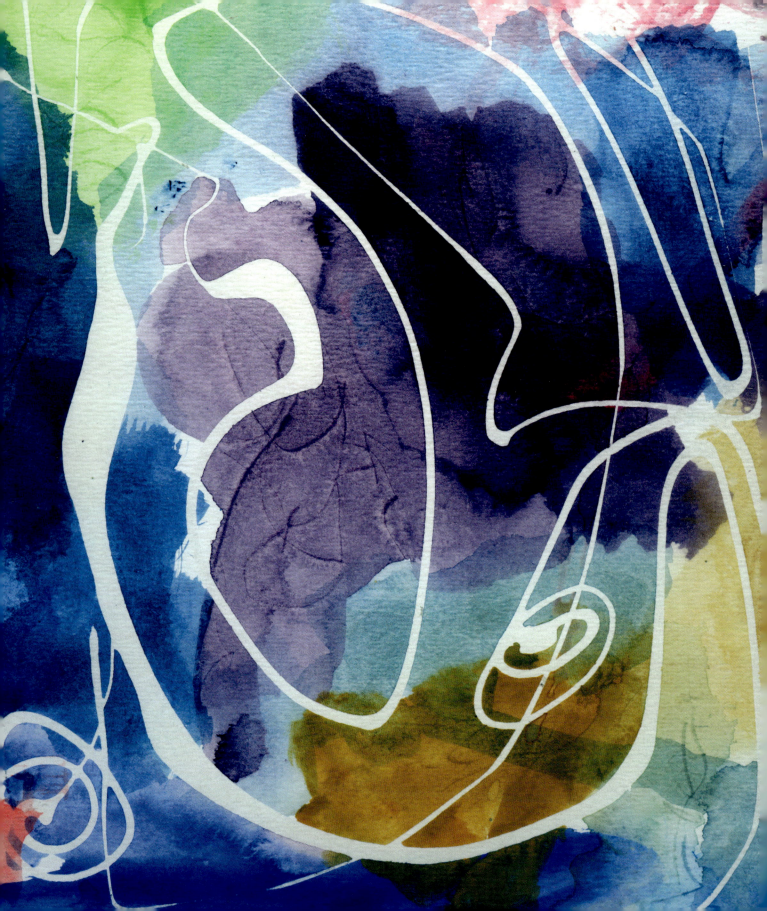

Many who know Judy will be surprised that she describes her inner life so succinctly. They associate her with her outward manifestations: hesitancy in speech and an anxiousness because few give her the time to express herself in words.

This book was begun in 1995 and developed in the following way: Once a week, Pauline Paulin, a devoted and dedicated long-time volunteer, worked with Judy on her writing. Judy would provide a title and then dictate a paragraph or two on that theme. Pauline typed up Judy's writing and sent it to me. I sorted out the subjects under major group headings and edited to eliminate repetition, choosing the best sentences for expressing themes that Judy repeatedly wrote about. Working in this way, her thoughts emerged in a coherent stream. From her wheelchair she intensely observed the life around her, and her situation provided her over many years with insights and a personal philosophy that will be an inspiration to many.

Once Judy discovered that she could hold a brush and learn to paint, in 1996, her self-expression knew no bounds. She felt herself to be a functioning member of society, with responsibility for her thoughts and actions. Her body is limited, but her mind is not. There are many others in this situation who need an opening for self-expression. Who knows what gifts lie inside the limitations of a body! This brings to mind Judy's own words, "Don't judge us by the outside," a profound spiritual adjunct, and one, it is hoped, that will be observed as persons with disabilities ("rolling people") come to be seen as the same on the inside as you and me, and a powerful group to be recognized as legislation extends their rights and liberties.

I met Judy one day in late 1992 after my own book was published. I had been invited to the institution where Judy lived to meet another resident. Having arrived early, I was unpre-

MY BOOK

I HOPE MY BOOK HELPS PEOPLE, BUT I KNOW I DON'T HAVE ALL THE ANSWERS. I DON'T EVEN HAVE ALL THE QUESTIONS.

THE WIND BLOWS THE SAME FOR EVERYONE AND IT WHISPERS IN OUR EARS. YOU CAN'T SEE THE WIND, ONLY THE EFFECTS OF ITS PRESENCE.

SOME PEOPLE ACT LIKE THEY DON'T SEE ME, BUT I HOPE IN THIS BOOK THEY WILL SEE THE EFFECTS OF MY LIFE.

pared for the large number of people in wheelchairs that I encountered. Uneasily I began backing out of the doorway, deciding to wait for my contacts outside. But Judy, sitting in the hallway, cheerily asked me if she could help. We began to talk, and she told me she wrote poetry. We discussed that and she asked for my business card. She also asked if I could visit her. Several weeks went by. Judy called one Sunday to remind me of my promise. So, on my way to a walk at the beach, I stopped by. After talking a while, Judy asked me if I could wheel her outside to the garden. I did. Then a little later, she asked if I could take her to the end of the driveway. I did. After that, she asked if I could take her to the traffic lights. I did. And when we were at the lights, she asked if I could take her to the beach. I was open to that too. Not knowing that she had to sign out whenever she left her place, we set off along the edge of the busy street on a hot summer afternoon towards the beach, about a mile away. The road was level and when we arrived, Judy had enough money to buy a hot chocolate—I had left my belongings in my parked car. We stayed until it got cooler, then made the journey back to the institution, past the tall grasses growing along the roadside and following the rim of the mountains with our eyes. From that encounter on, Judy associated me with adventures, and we had many.

I have been Judy's advocate from 1992, helping her expand her world, despairing with her when she wanted to move out into the community and it seemed there was no way, encouraging her to write and paint and express herself. It has been a shared journey of bumps and smooth places, sorrows and joys. This book is Judy's tribute to herself, the expression of her thoughts, longings, fears, feelings and emotions, and also the sharing of her life so that others in similar circumstances can realize that despite physical limitations, a great deal can be accomplished.

MKD

White Series No. 8, watercolor on paper

*S*ometimes I wonder why God made me this way. Could I be a mistake? Does God make mistakes?

I do believe that there's a power greater than myself in the universe, and this I call God. I don't know if this is the same God that the churches teach. I've had my problems with churches, preachers, and church people, but I still have a basic belief in God, and I'm searching for more light on this subject. I try to believe in heaven, hell and sin, but I'm not sure I can. I've heard so many different views that conflict with one another, and it's hard to make sense of it.

Once a church said that I had demons because I was disabled. I was shocked and wondered if it could be true. The people asked if they could pray for me and ask God to chase away the demons causing my condition. After an hour I was not cured, and they said that it was because I had no faith! I felt embarrassed and ashamed. I left the house of God worse off than I had entered. This happened to me several times. I felt it was my fault. I was devastated! I've learned that I have to sep-arate my disappointment in people from my faith in God. God is right on time with healing. It may be on this earth or in eternity.

I would like to be closer to God. I pray privately from time to time. I wish God would appear to me, talk to me, explain things to me, love me. I'm not opposed to Him, but it sure

---

THOUGHTS ON GOD

A MOUNTAIN HAS STRENGTH, HEIGHT, BEAUTY, COLOR, SHAPE, MAJESTY, POWER.

BECAUSE MY CREATOR IS GENEROUS AND GREAT, THROUGH HIM I WILL BE LIKE A MOUNTAIN.

Judy as a baby with her mother, 1942. Used with permission.

---

upsets me that He chooses to be so distant. Why won't He show Himself?

When God the Maker looks at a person, he doesn't look at the outside—it's the heart of the person He cares about. Outward appearances are for man's eyes; inward appearances are for God's eyes. God gives us life. It's our choice which path we follow. The truth is divine—nothing satisfies me but the truth.

Inside everyone is a little voice that talks to you and tells you to listen. In the fifties, when I was very sick after an experimental operation on my legs, this voice inside me told me that I would get better...and I did. Listening to the voice put peace inside, even though I felt a lot of pain. If you are quiet and listen to the still small voice inside, it will tell you what to do.

I don't know if there is an afterlife, but I like to think that there are flowers and sunshine and that it would be a pretty place. And no wheelchairs. People who loved you before and who you loved would be able to see you again. I like to think that our friends who have died can see us and hear us. Maybe the afterlife is coming back in a different form. I would like (if I had the choice) to come back as a bird, so I can watch over people.

I believe that someone made me for a reason, because I've been through a lot.

Song of the Sky, watercolor on paper

Being different from others is normal. All people have differences. Each person is unique.

My difference is being in a wheelchair, but I'm not different in the way I think and feel and what I like to do. I can't run or play ball, but I like to watch others who do. People think that when I'm with them, they have to do something special with me, but I don't have to be entertained. I enjoy just watching and being with people.

I wish I could walk. That's most important. I wish I could use my hands better. I wish I didn't need a wheelchair. I'm not feeling sorry for myself. This is a true fact. I wish people would see our likenesses and overlook our differences. I wish people would accept me as a normal person. I want them to forget I'm disabled.

"Normal" is defined by where a person is. In some places, hot days are normal. In other places, cold days are normal. What is normal about people is where they are. Some people think normal people are those who can walk. But where I live, the normal person can't walk. So we are all normal in some respect.

I am normal in lots of ways. I wrote this book. I paint. I listen to books on tape. I try to help others. I have desires and thoughts. I laugh and I cry and I get upset, just like you.

WHAT IS NORMAL?

I'll Help Them

IF I ONLY HAD TWO ARMS THAT HOLD,
I WOULD OF COURSE BE VERY BOLD,
I WOULD BE READY FOR ANY TASK
THAT ANY FRIEND WOULD EVER ASK.

IF I ONLY HAD TWO LEGS THAT RUN,
I WOULD DO ERRANDS FOR EVERYONE,
AND THIS WOULD MAKE ME HAPPY INDEED,
BECAUSE I'D BE HELPING THOSE IN NEED.

AND THOUGH THESE THINGS ARE HARD FOR ME,
TO EVERYONE, A FRIEND I'LL BE,
I'LL HELP THEM ALL, SO THEY MAY SEE
THAT THEY NEED HELP TOO, JUST LIKE ME.

I don't always get what I want—that's the way it is. I have moods. I have days that are up and down. I have days when I'm happy.

I hope I can live in a house like other people do, and have good neighbors, and I could have friends over. I want to be as independent as I can be.

People sometimes don't understand what I say. I cannot control the volume of my voice. They avoid me because of fear, and they think I'll bother them. I really hate that. I wish people would talk to me—I wonder why they don't. I don't want to feel like an untouchable, like being in a wheelchair is fearful just because it's different.

I want people to know that I have feelings, just like they do. I can feel when they don't like me or if they're ignoring me or don't want to be near me. I'd like to do the same things everybody else does. When friends include me with their friends and family, it makes me feel happy. I'm really just like anybody else.

If you can find a definition of what a normal person is, please tell me, because I don't think there is such a thing. I think it's the way you feel about yourself and the way you treat others. Everyone thinks that "normal" is something different, so whatever you think it is, it is. It's a controversial subject.

Opposite: Longing, watercolor on paper
Reflection, watercolor on paper

I do not want other people con-trolling my life. I do not want "Uncle Sam" controlling me. I do not want my family to control me. I belong to me. Who I am and what I have are mine. No one should be able to control me. I want to come or go, to move or stay in one place, spend or save, sleep or stay up as I choose. I want to be my own person.

I feel like I'm stuck—my family controls so much. It's like they have me captive. They shouldn't do that to me because I'm an adult and I should be in control of my own life. At first I hoped my family would treat me like a capable adult, but they never did. When I invite them to events, they rarely come. Some of my friends are more like family than my family. I'm not invited to visit my brother's house, or my mother's when she had a home. So I feel left out. My time with my family is not quality time. They rush away. I realize they're busy. I'm not complaining. I just want to be part of the family. It seems that they only visit me because they feel they have to.

I want to live like a normal person, away from this place and other places like it. I'm an adult and smart and I should be treated like I'm smart, not treated like a retarded person. Why do my family tell me what to do with my life? They are scared for me if I move out. But I tell them that it will be all right. I can be safe. What's wrong with needing help with your body? I

A LIFE WITH CONTROLS

RIDING THE ROLLER COASTER

UP, UP, UP I GO! I HEAR THE CHAIN CLICKING. MY STOMACH IS CHURNING. THEN, WITHOUT WARNING—DOWN, DOWN, DOWN. TWISTING AND TURNING, MY STOMACH IN MY FEET! NEVER SURE WHAT'S COMING NEXT. NOT IN CONTROL OF THE RIDE.

IT'S WEIRD, EXCITING, AND SCARY.

UP, UP, UP MY HOPES AND EXPECTATIONS GO. THE CHAIN OF LIFE IS CLICKING. MY STOMACH IS UPSET, WONDERING HOW LONG IT WILL BE BEFORE MY HOPES ARE DASHED. THEN, WITHOUT WARNING—DOWN, DOWN, DOWN, INTO DEPRESSION AND HOPELESSNESS. TWISTING AND TURNING WITH EVERY LETTER THE GOVERNMENT SENDS, STOMACH IN MY FEET! NEVER SURE WHAT'S COMING NEXT. NOT IN CONTROL OF MY ROLLER COASTER LIFE.

IT'S WEIRD, WILD, AND SCARY AS HELL.

---

know a lot of people who need help with their bodies, but are still able to do what they want to do.

You know, I have my own voice, but sometimes I don't use it because I'm afraid I will get in trouble. I want people to listen to my voice. I want to be able to make decisions about my own life. I don't want people to make decisions for me or develop programs for me. I want to control my life. I know how to create things to do for myself, but I need help to accomplish my goals.

Living in this environment, you are supposed to be able to make your own choices. But it doesn't seem like that. Even in a smaller institution, I feel that it wouldn't be different. I am told: You cannot use your hands to write, or you cannot use your hands enough to pass legal requirements for financial reasons. I have a stamp now for my signature—before, I couldn't make it legible enough to be accepted. And I am told: If you have to have things read to you, you can't live on your own. I can read big print, but it's hard because I have dyslexia. I feel that I don't have any say in choices that affect me.

When I take medicine, I would like to know more about the side effects. If I don't want to take the medication, I shouldn't have to. Doctors should tell me what they are doing and why. When I hurt a rib and asked about my injury, they only said, "Try to continue to do everything that you were doing." I should at least know what's going on.

White Series No. 9, watercolor on paper

I was born in Evanston, Illinois in 1942, but the way people treat me sometimes, you'd think I was from Mars. I've checked the mirror, but I don't see antennae on my head. What's so strange about me? My wheelchair isn't an alien spaceship! What are people afraid of? Maybe the fact that my body is different makes them believe I'm from some other planet. I'm just a simple girl from Planet Earth. I want what every other girl wants—to be liked, to be connected, to belong.

When people see me in my wheelchair they assume that I'm not capable. Nothing could be further from the truth. I'm a strong and capable female who wants a chance to prove it. I have certain limitations, but who doesn't! I'm a hard worker. I'm confident and courageous. I'm not afraid to fight or work for what I want. It's my life, and I intend to live it fully. I want to be helpful to all people and I hope they will be helpful to me. You can either help me or at least get out of my way, because I'm coming through. I will not be denied.

Self-esteem is learning to value yourself. As a disabled person, it's not easy. You get lots of put-downs and it can make

---

THE GIRL FROM MARS

FOLLOW YOUR HEART

FOLLOW YOUR HEART WHERE IT LEADS,
EVEN IF IT ACHES AND BLEEDS;
OVER THE OBSTACLES, THROUGH THE DARK,
ALWAYS FOLLOW YOUR HEART.

FOLLOW YOUR HEART WHERE IT LEADS,
HELPING OTHER PEOPLE WITH NEEDS;
GIVE OF YOURSELF, YOUR INNER PART—
WHATEVER HAPPENS, FOLLOW YOUR HEART.

---

you feel bad about yourself. You must learn—whoever you are—that you are worthy and important. I've been working on my self-esteem for years and I still have work to do, but I'm much more self-aware than I used to be. Whoever you are, you are somebody! Quit listening to negative people and realize your own specialness!

Some people seem to think I should be cheerful all the time, I should be happy and smiling. Maybe they think that because I'm in a wheelchair and live where I have things done for me that I can't do, that I don't have worries like the rest of the world. The truth is I have the same worries as any other human being. So if I'm not cheerful all the time, I might be thinking of one of my worries.

Don't look at my wheelchair— look at me. I am a normal human being. I am not a spectacle. Therefore, don't think weird things about me. Don't say things that will bring me down. Be a part of my life—be my friend. Accept my wheelchair as part of me, because it is part of me. Don't say harsh things about me or rude things, as it isn't kind. I look up to others, therefore I expect them to do the same to me.

Don't look down on me!

Opposite: Follow Your Heart, watercolor on paper
Passion, watercolor on paper

There are walking sticks made of wood—that's not the kind I'm thinking of. Imagine walking sticks made of love! When someone needs support, you reach out to them with your walking stick.

Once you're born, you're always looking for love. Everyone needs to be loved by someone. Sometimes I feel that nobody loves me or cares about me. It feels so terrible when I think no one can understand my tears.

Walking people seem to receive more love than rolling people. In reality, rolling people know how to give love, if people would just let them.

I want to be loved for who I am. Love makes me feel good, like I'm a person. Love gives me life, makes me feel better about myself. Everyone has the potential to love or be loved, but it can't happen in isolation. Take time for friendship—it's an important part of love. When you help somebody and don't want anything back, that shows your love.

Understanding each other is love, no matter what the situation. Helping each other makes us grow. Breaking down barriers and opening ourselves up is one way of understanding. I don't let my wheelchair or my body limit me. I want to show my love for the whole human race.

WALKING STICKS OF LOVE

DISCUSSION, NOT ARGUMENT,
LOVE INSTEAD OF HATE,
SELFLESSNESS, NOT SELF-CENTEREDNESS
OR NARROW-MINDEDNESS,
GIVING INSTEAD OF TAKING,
CAN INSTEAD OF CAN'T,
GOOD FEELINGS REPLACING BAD FEELINGS.
AN OPEN MIND.
WALLS WOULD TUMBLE DOWN,
HOPE, NOT DESPAIR.
NEGATIVE TO POSITIVE.

Bad feelings need to be worked out, or they will limit you and ruin your life. This is true for all people. We need to be able to listen to each other, and not be judgmental.

Love is "regardless of," and not "because of." If we love someone because they say and do things we like, there is a good chance we are not coming from a place of loving, but from a place of approving. This is because the person says and does things we already accept.

True love is accepting each other regardless, when you love someone even though that person does things that you can't stand. True love is loving someone who may look a little different, or may need a little extra assistance in getting around and doing things. If people would just say "I love you" and mean it, the world would be a happier place.

There are matters of the mind and matters of the heart—two very different things. I don't "think" my way to help those less fortunate—I use my heart. I feel compassion and that motivates me to action. Too many people deal only with matters of the mind. I have chosen weightier matters—matters of the heart.

Do you have a walking stick of love? Reach out with it and help someone.

Blossoms, watercolor on paper
Opposite: Love, watercolor on paper

Those in charge say that they protect the disabled from themselves. If the disabled want to do something different or risky, they're stopped. It's for their own good, they say. Who decides? When does protection become imprisonment?

Sometimes, the loneliness and separation make me feel like I'm alone on an island. No one to turn to. No one who really understands. Just me, on the shore looking out to sea. Some say my struggle is over, but I say my struggle is never over. The struggle of life lasts as long as a heart still beats. In life, there is a constant struggle for power, money, and fame. For me, a struggle for survival, independence, and freedom is raging.

I struggle against rules, like State rules. There are rules for everything under the sun. Most of them are ridiculous. The State says that if I work hard and make money, then they will cut off my support. Why do we have laws that discourage creativity and independence among the disabled? How can I get my share of the "American Dream"?

The System—did it pass me by? Yes, it certainly did—just like I wasn't even there. I want to get out and I can't. It's so big and impersonal—I'm just a number.

PROTECTION OR PRISON?

LIFE IS A CAGE!
NO, IT'S A CAGE WITHIN A CAGE.
NO, THAT'S NOT IT EITHER.
LIFE IS A CAGE WITHIN A CAGE
WITHIN A CAGE.

IF A PERSON COULD SOMEHOW
ESCAPE THE FIRST CAGE, IT'S NO GOOD,
BECAUSE THEY HAVE ONLY MANAGED
TO ESCAPE INTO THE NEXT CAGE.
IF THEY ESCAPE THAT CAGE,
THERE'S ALWAYS ANOTHER CAGE.
IN OTHER WORDS,
THERE IS NO ESCAPE.

SOMETIMES IT SEEMS THAT WAY TO ME.

Oh, the paperwork! It seems like there is paperwork for everything. You have to sign papers to put your pictures on the wall! You have to sign papers to go to school! All these papers drive me crazy. Before long, you'll have to sign paperwork to go to the bathroom or to breathe.

In any place like this you have limited choices about what you can and cannot do. It's not like a regular life where you have lots of choices. The System tells you when to eat and what to eat. In a group home you have a menu and that's it, the same thing for everyone. Sometimes the way the food is presented makes you want to eat out.

Self-advocacy is a movement that has no power. Society gives the disabled a so-called "voice," but really nothing in the way of real changes in policy occurs. It isn't normal for a large group of disabled people to live together—one disabled person with their aide or one disabled person with their family is the way it should be. It's society herding its weakest members together into groups that they can hide away and forget exist.

Why does my every activity, every move, have to be written down in a book for the State to see? Is that normal? What if every able-bodied person had a book kept to record their every deed? Do you think they would allow it to continue?

Dark Clouds, watercolor on paper

People in programming and the staff at my residence talk a lot about behavior. Do they set a good example? Why are they so hard on us, telling us what to do? What about me? I know what I want to do for my own program. However, they act like I don't have any brains. I feel that they might take advantage of me, like telling me the wrong time so that I have to go to bed earlier than I normally would.

White Series No. 12, watercolor on paper
Opposite: White Series No. 19, watercolor on paper

Sometimes, I feel like my life has been roadblocked. No matter which way I go, there is something or someone in my way. If I back up, there's something behind me. If I go sideways, there's a fence. It really makes me frustrated! It's one thing not to help me, but quite another to set up roadblocks. Why would so many people be so interested in me not getting where I want to go? Don't they have anything better to do? Some even set up roadblocks and tell me it's because they care. I'm strong, and I'll keep on moving until I break through every roadblock that keeps me from my dreams.

Twice a year I have a meeting called an IPP (Individual Program Plan). This has been going on for many years, maybe as many as thirty-five. The purpose of the meeting is to discuss my situation, what I'm doing, and what my plans are. The idea behind the IPP is good—to help me do what I want to do. But what I want to do never seems to happen.

I don't blame anybody. I know that people are trying, but it just seems like nothing never happens. Maybe we should call it "Nothing Never Happens" instead of IPP. The focus is on my physical therapy. That's okay, but my biggest concerns are about getting out of here and on my own.

These meetings are so repetitive, I know all the questions and answers before I even go to the meeting. Take this example: For as long as I can remember, I have wanted to take action to move into my own apartment. Twenty-five years after my initial discussion, my next IPP report stated: "Judy's main concern continues to be to move out and into an apartment of her own."

Guess what! Everybody already knows that. It's no secret. However, there's always some reason why my dream can't be fulfilled. It seems that I have the necessary skills—being able to organize finances, hire aides, and express my needs—but nothing never happens.

And what about my electric chair? Given the choice of being a stationary "roller" or a rolling "roller," wouldn't you prefer to be mobile? However, my electric chair is not safe. I've broken my toes many times and my wrist when the chair tipped or I bumped into something. If it can be made safe for me, I'll try it again.

NOTHING NEVER HAPPENS

WAYS TO HELP PEOPLE

SMILE AND OTHERS WILL SMILE BACK.
REAL KINDNESS IS DOING SOMETHING FOR
SOMEONE ELSE WITHOUT COMPLAINING
OR GRUMBLING
OR SAYING THAT WE ARE IN THE WAY.

I want to talk about finances but I'm told they don't know what money I'll get from Social Security, so we're stuck. The money doesn't seem enough to cover what I want to do.

People point out my weaknesses, but why don't they ever mention my strengths? The more people talk about what I can't do, the harder it becomes for me to think positively. I have many strengths that go unnoticed. If people are here to help me, why not help me focus on strengths? Everyone has their weaknesses and I'm no different, but focusing on them leads nowhere. Let's shake off all this negative talk and look at what can be done.

So much of what happens here seems like political nonsense. They fill out forms, have meetings, and tell the government we're doing what we're supposed to. Is anyone learning anything? Is anyone really becoming independent? Year after year, everything seems the same. Change the faces, change the forms, but it's the same game. Why can't they cut the political crap and find legitimate ways of helping us?

Why is it okay for a so-called "able-bodied" person to be angry? Or to have a behavior that is different? We have feelings, likes and dislikes and opinions, but if we express them, then right off, oh my, someone says we have a behavior problem and we need a psychologist or a tranquilizer. They just don't understand the frustration.

The person studying my case for my IPP put down some issue I needed to work on, like interrupting. I may have this problem, but so do other people. I feel singled out, like things I say are wrong. I feel people in charge don't listen to me. So when I interrupt, I get called down. There is fear that if a disabled person gets too assertive or demanding, we worry

about whether anyone will care for our needs. If you say you don't like something your caregiver is doing, maybe they will cut back your care.

Some of the programming people are nice, but others tell you all the things that you do wrong. This is most apparent during the IPP meetings. I like the meetings to be as short as possible, so there's less time to say bad things. I always hear how much worse I'm getting. Maybe they don't realize this, but that's what they do. It makes me angry and it hurts me. Suppose these people could trade places with me. How would they like it if they were like me? They need to "walk in my shoes" for a while. They don't know how it is, they just think they do. They might become sympathetic and have more patience. A new atmosphere could be created. They might understand my feelings better and realize how important it is to hear good things about yourself.

There are things that I think are possible for me to accomplish and I have made them personal goals. I want to be a famous painter and I want to live in my own home. Some people smile or say, "You can do it, Judy," but I think they really mean, "It's impossible, Judy." They just say it to make me feel good. I know I'll need help, but I think my goal is possible. It was possible for others.

Opposite: Despair, watercolor on paper
A Tree for Xmas, watercolor on paper

When I was nine years old I was put into an institution. I didn't want to go, but my family thought it was best for me. That's the first time I felt abandoned. Several years later I went into the hospital for experimental surgery and came out having to stay mostly in bed for three years. I felt abandoned again. Now I feel it when people say they will help me and then they don't. Abandoned!

When I begin to develop relationships with others, it starts with visits, dinners, and lots of sharing. I accept or suggest activities and find much enjoyment doing them with my friends, who become a large part of my life. Then it ends.

Something happens to make them too busy, or they change their minds. I'm never sure why. Visits are fewer and further between. The activities become rare. Sometimes I suggest doing something together, but am confronted with a barrier. I am left with no options. Our friendship is over unless they contact me.

Families start off broken-hearted at the thought of sending their loved ones off to an institution. In the early days, frequent visits are made. Slowly the State takes over and the families

FAMILIES OFF THE HOOK

I'M ANGRY WHEN I'M NOT TREATED LIKE A NORMAL PERSON. PEOPLE DON'T UNDERSTAND WHAT IT'S LIKE TO BE ME. I GET HURT WHEN THEY SAY I CAN'T DO THIS, OR I CAN'T GO THERE, JUST BECAUSE I'M IN A WHEELCHAIR. THEY LOOK AT THE WHEELCHAIR AND THINK I DON'T HAVE A BRAIN. I FEEL LEFT OUT OF THEIR LIVES.

*Judy with her brother, ca 1949.
Used with permission.*

retreat. Over time, no one expects much from the families. The State cares for the disabled and the families are off the hook.

I love my family but they don't visit too often. If I call on the phone, they'll talk a little. They discuss the possibility of coming, then someone says, "No use to upset her, she's happy there in her own little world."

My family doesn't include me in their activities. I believe it is because I'm too much trouble. Their house is inaccessible and there's not enough room for me. I embarrass them in public because I'm different.

I am not really that different—I want the same things other people do. I don't want to be in the way. How can I feel OK about myself when everyone else is saying by their attitude that I'm not OK. My self-image is hard to keep positive when this self seems so negative to others.

I want to live in an environment that is less isolated. I want more integration with the general society and to be able to work alongside other people. I want to make a difference and feel like there is a purpose to my life. I need to have a reason why we were sent here and why we must deal with life. I need to have a reason to live.

Winter, watercolor on paper

Although sometimes I've felt down and out and thought I couldn't go on, I've always somehow found the strength to continue. Every time I've been knocked down, I get back up and keep going. Sometimes I feel cold and cynical, but even then, I keep my courage and move ahead. I will always keep going. I will always keep growing, no matter what!

Dreaming is comforting. When you're dreaming, you can go anywhere. You can laugh, you can fly—you can do anything. Dreams can come true; just hold on to them! When you dream, you are letting your spirit free, especially during the difficult times of your life.

When I was born, nobody knew the physical difficulties that I would have in my future. I can face the reality that I am challenged for life, and I can choose to hold my head up high.

People need to keep an open mind because they never know what can happen to them in life. Life is unpredictable. What is needed are better listening skills. If you have ideas

LOSING YOUR IDENTITY

FEAR IS THE GREATEST ENEMY. WE TOGETHER
CAN CHANGE FALSE FEARS.
EVERYTHING, EVERYONE—WE ARE ALL
HERE AND RECOGNIZABLE.
EVERYONE IS IDENTIFIABLE AND
OF WORTH AND VALUE.
MY SAMENESS MAY BE HARD FOR OTHERS
TO SEE, AND IF SEEN, TO ACCEPT.
HOW CAN, DOES, A PERSON IN A WHEELCHAIR
REACT TO THIS ATTITUDE?
PERHAPS WE RETREAT.

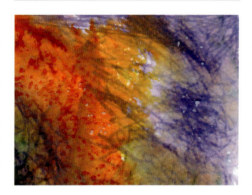

about people before you listen to them, it affects how you listen. This is prejudice.

People who cannot function mentally and physically can tend to lose their identity. If I am prevented from interacting with people who can walk around, then I can only interact with rolling people like myself. We should be able to interact with everybody. Otherwise, we are not included as citizens of the community and society.

Is it right to judge others? Is it right for others to judge me? No! To judge others is like breaking a law of humanity. People need to know that the only way you can become disabled is through an accident, early or later in life. And let me stress that (1) we can't help it, and (2) you cannot catch it.

Many disabled people can't speak for themselves. I'm lucky because I can talk. I want to be their voice. I want to let the world know that they are people too. I want to make sure they aren't robbed of their rights.

Retreat, watercolor on paper
Opposite: Courage, String Series, watercolor on paper

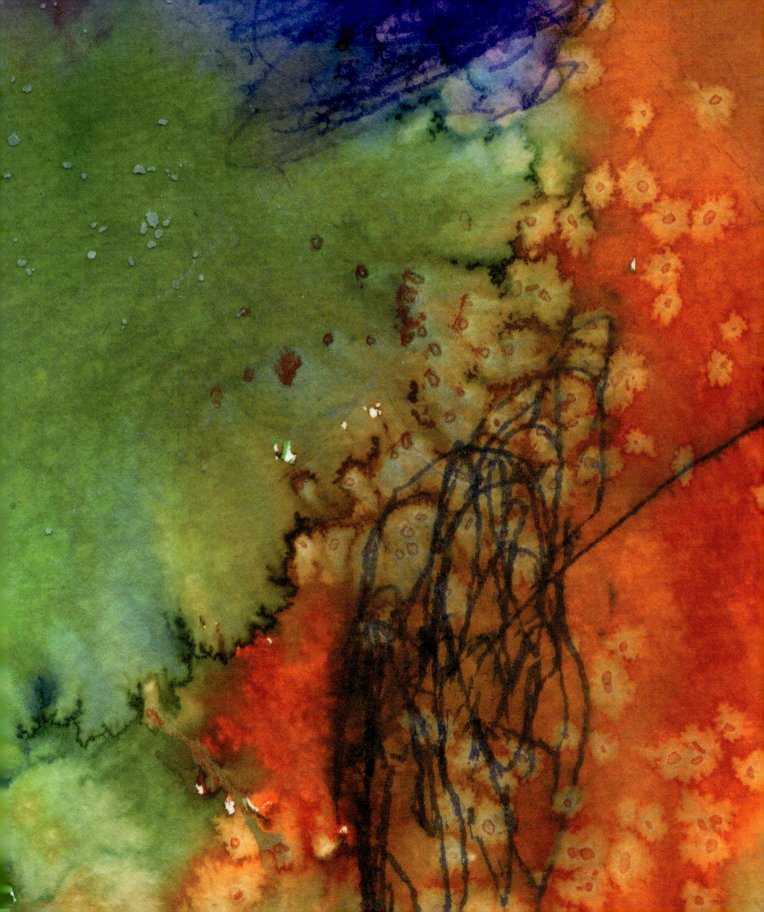

I started painting watercolors in April 1996. A craft teacher at the institution put a paintbrush in my hand. I didn't know what to do. I started making strong circles. I learned to paint by myself. Sometimes I make mistakes—my hand doesn't always do what I want it to. But it usually turns out pretty good.

Painting releases a lot of tension. It makes me feel like I'm doing something for myself. It's easy to learn how to paint, though maybe not at first.

I'm taking three art classes a week at Adult Ed. My teachers showed me different materials to use. I learned techniques, like leaving a little white in the picture. I learned paper has to be a certain heaviness. You can use different paints to make different effects. I like painting where I can make a design by myself, or I can change it if I want to. You have to use special watercolor brushes to hold water. I did some canvases with acrylic paints too, and I'd like to learn other methods. You can make a dry design or a wet one—you can have the design in your mind and make it up on the paper, or make it random. If it doesn't look good, you can cover it up and do it again.

People in the art class are helpful. One person cut mats for my pictures. Another put shrinkwrap around the paintings to protect them and to look more professional. In summer, with no classes, I paint on my own.

PAINTING IS MY THERAPY

"*ART AS THERAPY* BOLDLY PROPOSES THAT ART HAS A CLEAR FUNCTION: IT IS A THERAPEUTIC TOOL TO HELP US LEAD MORE FULFILLED LIVES."

FROM THE BOOK *ART AS THERAPY* BY ALAIN DE BOTTON AND JOHN ARMSTRONG

Going to Sausalito several times were important trips. More people saw my work. I passed out my cards in Margaret's studio. Everyone in the ICB building was showing their work. I sold a few things. Having my art on exhibit made me feel good about myself. It made me feel important. I felt free. I felt on my way toward accomplishing my goals and becoming independent.

I've had group shows in Santa Barbara, and I'm a member of the Los Padres Watercolor Society. I'd like to get to know some Santa Barbara artists besides my teachers and the people in my classes.

I enjoy using my mind in those long hours in my wheelchair. I love colors, paints, beauty and art. Someday I'll work in my own studio and be in big art shows. For now I keep on painting day and night. I work hard, without many breaks. It's the one thing that helps me get through the tedium of every long day.

Whenever I can get someone to set me up with my apron, brush, paints and paper, I paint. I paint to relax. I paint to escape boredom. I paint to relieve depression. It doesn't matter if the paintings are good to anyone else—they are therapy to me. I get so involved with my painting that I don't have time to think about problems. Painting can work wonders in people's lives. I know—it's worked wonders in mine!

Opposite: Beyond the Horizon, watercolor on Japanese rice paper
Bouquet, watercolor on paper

*Our slender life runs quickly by,
into the silent night and gone!
My life is like a piece of dust in the
wind, whirling round and round and
where it lands, who knows?*

How can we know what's out there? No one comes back to tell us. One story sounds as good as the next. How can we know for sure? What train are we on? Who's driving? Is the bridge out? Where is the train headed? Do you have a ticket? Do I need a ticket? Are you trying to sell me a ticket? If you are right, is nobody wrong? How many answers are there to a simple question? Am I crazy? Who are you to say! Can you prove you're not? How can we know?

The present moment is the most important and precious resource I have. The past is gone. The future isn't here yet.

OUR SLENDER LIFE

DANCE OF LIFE

THERE IS A DANCE IN THE OCEAN'S WAVES,
THERE IS A SONG THAT EACH SOUL CRAVES;

THE WIND IS DANCING IN THE TREES,
THE SONG OF LIFE IS DANCING IN ME.

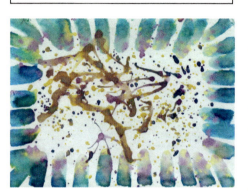

This moment—right now—writing these words, is everything. You—right now—reading this, is everything. If I write things that matter, then my present moment is well spent. If you, the reader, spend your present moment reading what I have written, the moment will connect us.

Life is like a play—different characters acting according to a script. It would be much easier to properly play my part if I had a copy of the script. The director always seems to be busy somewhere else. People make different rules, telling you what to do and what not to do when you're in a place like this. Things keep happening and I don't know why. I would like to write my own part. I believe I know what it is. I'm here to help others and to be helped by them. I guess I have two parts.

White Series No. 20, watercolor on paper
Opposite: White Series No. 5, watercolor on paper

In February 2001, supporters formed the Judy Gilder Independent Living Support Group. In October 2002, Judy had the opportunity to present her desire for a home in the community at the Olmstead Forum, sponsored by the ILRC and Area Agency on Aging. With Judy beside her, Margaret Kay Dodd read Judy's statement. Excerpts follow.

"Statement on behalf of Judy Gilder, an artist and writer who is disabled, who has lived in the same institution for 51 years, and desires to move away from institutional living and into the community, as is her right by law.

The Olmstead Decision, in 1999, ruled that unnecessary segregation of persons with disabilities in institutions is a form of discrimination in violation of the Americans with Disabilities Act (ADA), which requires that persons with disabilities receive services in the most integrated settings. This decision and the Lanterman Act support the legal rights of the developmentally disabled, which include the right of self-determination and being able to choose where one lives, who one lives with, where and with whom one can work, and how one can spend one's leisure time....'

"Judy Gilder will be 61 next January. She came to live at the institution at the age of nine, in 1950. Captive against her will in a body, a facility, and a system over which she has no control, she eventually found an outlet for her energies in 1996 when she began painting, and a few years before that, as a writer. She and I have been working on a book about *how it is* and *how it feels* to be disabled. Her hope is that this book, titled

Freedom, watercolor on paper

AM I MY OWN?

THIS QUESTION MAY SOUND SILLY TO SOME. THEY MAY SAY, "OF COURSE YOU ARE YOUR OWN!" I BELIEVE IT'S A GOOD QUESTION FOR MYSELF AND OTHER DISABLED AMERICANS. OTHER PEOPLE DECIDE FOR ME IN MANY CASES, SOMETIMES GOING AGAINST MY DESIRES AND JUDGMENT. I HAVE A GOOD MIND. WHY AM I NOT MY OWN, JUST BECAUSE I AM DISABLED?

WHY ARE PEOPLE AFRAID ABOUT THIS MOVE? I'M NOT. I KNOW THAT PEOPLE WILL BE THERE FOR ME WHEN I REALLY NEED THEM. I KNOW HOW TO USE MY VOICE AND ASK FOR THINGS I NEED.

I HAVE PEOPLE THAT CARE ABOUT ME AS A PERSON. I HAVE AIDES THAT CARE ABOUT ME AS A PERSON, SO WHY SHOULD I BE AFRAID?

I WILL MAKE IT! AND I WILL MAKE IT AS GOOD AS THE REST WHO MADE IT, AND MAYBE EVEN BETTER.

DON'T WORRY. I WON'T GET BORED. I HAVE A WHOLE LOT OF THINGS TO DO.

From Where I Sit, will be one of advocacy for other people with disabilities, 'a voice for those who cannot speak.' Judy is a strong woman with clear objectives, and wishes to move forward in the direction she has chosen. She has done everything she knows how to structure a normal life within the confines of an institution.

"She started voicing a desire to live in the community over 25 years ago, when she recognized that there were other options for her in the world. She has watched as others have moved out into community apartments that were accessible, had support systems to make them successful, and had Section 8 funding. Almost all those who moved to a less restrictive environment that they chose came from the institution where Judy lives and similar facilities. Some had resided there for less time than Judy, and some had more significant disabilities and a higher level of care needs than Judy has—and yet she has 'fallen through the cracks' of the bureaucratic system...." Judy's "Am I My Own?" was then read.

After hearing the presentation, several professional people in the audience offered to assist Judy to realize her dream and became pivotal in its fulfilment. In early 2003, United Cerebral Palsy (UCP) completed the building of a group of pleasant cottages in an area with many amenities, and Judy was chosen to live there. Her joy was overwhelming, and in April 2003 she moved in. At last she could "choose the color of my towels" and begin to adjust to a different way of living.

It's been a couple of years since I moved out of an institution into my own apartment in April 2003. I'm happy now for the first time in my life. Life isn't as stressful as it once was. The institution was so noisy and impersonal and I never felt I was being treated like a normal human being. I felt just like a number. It wasn't anyone's fault. That's just the way institutions are.

When I first moved here I was so happy I didn't paint for a long time. Now I'm back to my painting. My new life has freed me up to take trips. I've been to Hawaii and Las Vegas and went on a cruise to Mexico. I'd like to go to Paris but I hear it is not a very wheelchair-accessible place.

Many people said I couldn't live on my own. For a while they had me doubting myself but I told them I wanted to do this and I did it. It was my last chance. I was determined to do it. I worked on moving out of an institution where I'd been for 52 years. It wasn't easy but with the help and support of a lot of people I did it. I never gave up. I'm doing great.

I love my privacy in my own place. I get more individual attention now and much better medical and personal care. I can still take art classes and choose to take other classes. I have a life now.

A lot of things about my own home are still kind of weird, especially around getting transportation. Perhaps someday I'll have my own van and a driver. But I'm not complaining about the difficulties. That's the way life is.

I hope this book will help other people. I want to be a living example of one person who never gave up. I did it and I'm still doing it! *(Written in 2005)*

Summer, watercolor on paper   *Opposite: Ocean Waves, watercolor on paper*

Opposite: New Day, String Series, watercolor on paper
Photo: Judy in Downtown Santa Barbara, 1995

judy's gallery

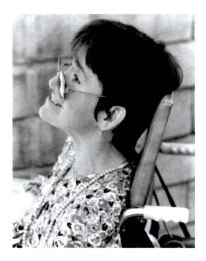

These paintings, all watercolor on paper, are not specifically dated, nor did Judy sign or title her work. Titles were suggested by her abstractions and supplied by Judy Nason and Margaret Kay Dodd. She is assisted to set up the watercolor paper, paints, and brushes on the tray of her wheelchair, and works from all four sides of a painting as the paper is turned for her. Being abstracts, her paintings can be viewed from any side, thus forming differing compositions. The dimensions of each painting are not given, but due to the limitation of movement of Judy's right hand and the size of the tray, paintings range from 4 x 6 inches to 11 x 14 inches. The *White Series* dates from ca. 2003; the *String Series* dates from ca. 2013; the *Pandemic Series* is dated 2020/2021. The paintings selected for this book were made from 1998 to 2021.

Cascade, String Series, watercolor on paper

Group Exhibitions, Marin, California

1996   ICB Winter Show, Sausalito

1997   ICB Winter Show, Sausalito; Marin Open Studios

1998   ICB Winter Show, Sausalito

Group Exhibitions, Santa Barbara, California

1998   Helping Hand Gallery

1999   Contemporary Arts Forum Open Exhibition; Became member of Los Padres Watercolor Society; Faulkner Gallery & Cabrillo Arts Pavilion with Los Padres Watercolor Society; Tri-Counties Regional Center: 1st Annual Art Exhibition at Alpha Resource Center, 2nd prize

2000   Faulkner Gallery & Cabrillo Arts Pavilion with Los Padres Watercolor Society; Santa Barbara Fair & Expo, 1st prize; Tri-Counties Regional Center: 2nd Annual Art Exhibition at the Ridley-Tree Art Center, 1st prize

2001   Faulkner Gallery & Cabrillo Arts Pavilion with Los Padres Watercolor Society; 1st Annual Canvas Project, The Arts Fund Gallery; Contemporary Arts Forum Open Exhibition; Santa Barbara Fair & Expo, 1st and 2nd prizes

2002   Faulkner Gallery & Cabrillo Arts Pavilion with Los Padres Watercolor Society; 2nd Annual Canvas Project, The Arts Fund Gallery; Santa Barbara Fair & Expo, 1st and 2nd prizes

2003   Faulkner Gallery & Cabrillo Arts Pavilion with Los Padres Watercolor Society; Antioch University 10th Annual Show, "Color Splash"; 3rd Annual Canvas Project, The Arts Fund Gallery; Santa Barbara Fair & Expo; Artist of the Month, Independent Living Resource Center; "A Tree for Xmas" painting used on official Xmas card for UCP (United Cerebral Palsy)

2004   Artist of the Month, Independent Living Resource Center; Faulkner Gallery & Cabrillo Arts Pavilion with Los Padres Watercolor Society; Santa Barbara Fair & Expo, 1st prize; 4th Annual Canvas Project, The Arts Fund Gallery; Jodi House Art Fair

2005   Santa Barbara Fair & Expo, 1st prize; Faulkner Gallery & Cabrillo Arts Pavilion with Los Padres Watercolor Society; Judy's painting hung in Santa Barbara Mayor's office to honor long-term residents of institutions who had moved into their own homes

2006   Tri-Counties Regional Center Group Show

2006 to 2017 *(annually)*

    Faulkner Gallery & Cabrillo Arts Pavilion with Los Padres Watercolor Society; Santa Barbara Fair & Expo

2016 *(ongoing)*

    Became member of Goleta Valley Art Association; Goleta Valley Art Association Group Shows

2020/2021 *(during the Covid pandemic)*

    Goleta Valley Art Association Virtual Online Gallery www.tgvaa.org/virtual-show

Publications

2020   *Goleta's Gazette*, Vol. 6, No, 8, May 1–16

2020   *Voice Magazine Santa Barbara*, August 21

2021   *Disability Truth: Central Coast Artists Commemorate the 30th Anniversary of the Americans with Disabilities Act* (A zine featuring nine of Judy's paintings plus text excerpts from her book, *From Where I Sit*), published by the ADA 30th Anniversary Committee, Santa Barbara, in January

Opposite: Sunlight, String Series, watercolor on paper
Spring, String Series, watercolor on paper

Radiance, watercolor on paper

Opposite: Crescent Moon, watercolor on paper

Opposite: Earth's Splendor, watercolor on paper
White Series No. 14, watercolor on paper

Sunset, watercolor on paper

Opposite: Fireworks, String Series, watercolor on paper

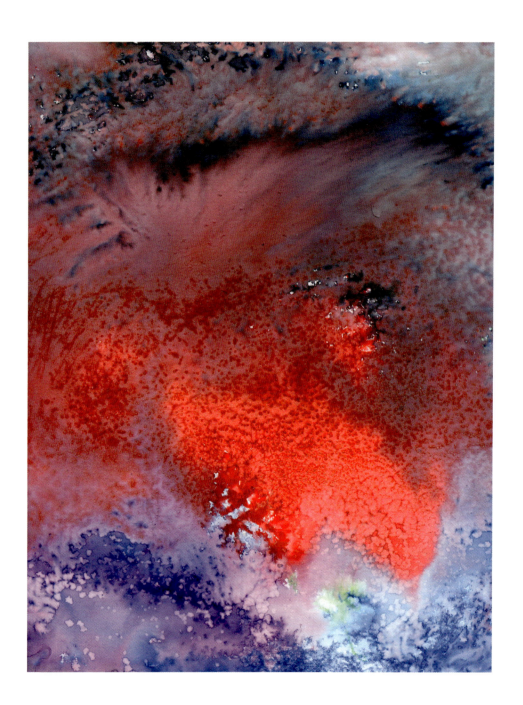

Opposite: Friendship, String Series, watercolor on paper
Breaking New Ground, watercolor on paper

Mystery, watercolor on paper
Opposite: Solar Wind, watercolor on paper

Opposite: Midnight, watercolor on paper
White Series No. 13, watercolor on paper

Destiny, watercolor on paper

Opposite: Fire in the Heart, watercolor on paper

Opposite: Gathering Storm, watercolor on paper
Facing the Unknown, watercolor on paper

Below the Sea, watercolor on paper
Opposite: Islands, watercolor on paper

Opposite:Web of Life I, watercolor on paper
Web of Life II, watercolor on paper

Cup of Gold, watercolor on paper

Opposite: Transition, watercolor on paper

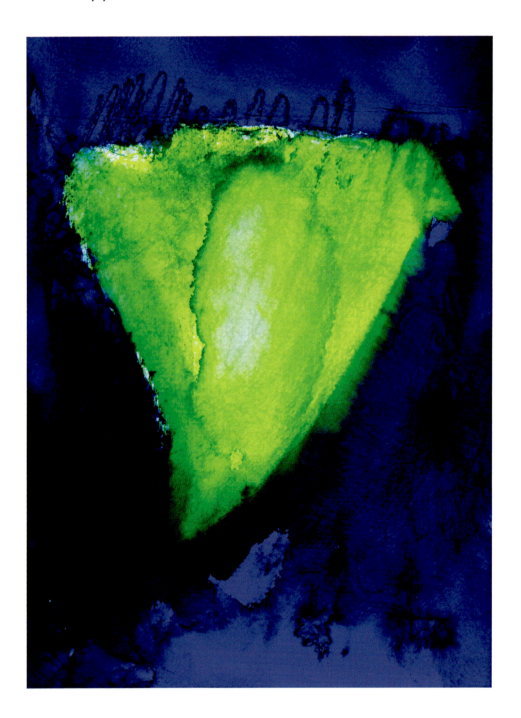

Opposite: Mardi Gras, watercolor on paper
Bright Waters, watercolor on paper

White Series No. 11, watercolor on paper
Opposite: Green Haven, watercolor on paper

Opposite: Facing Fear, watercolor on paper
Calligraphy with Thumbprints, watercolor on paper

Eclipse, watercolor on paper
Opposite: Sweet Dreams, watercolor on paper

Opposite: Kaleidoscope, watercolor on paper
Growth, watercolor on paper

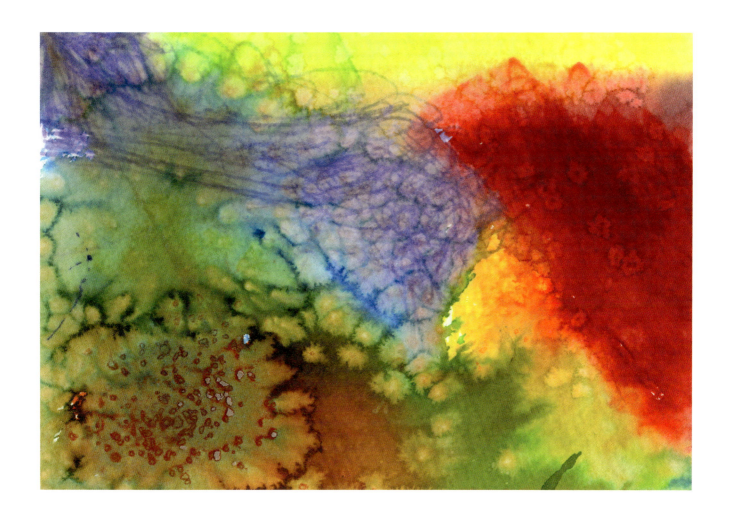

Autumn, watercolor on paper

Opposite: The Intricacies of Living, watercolor on paper

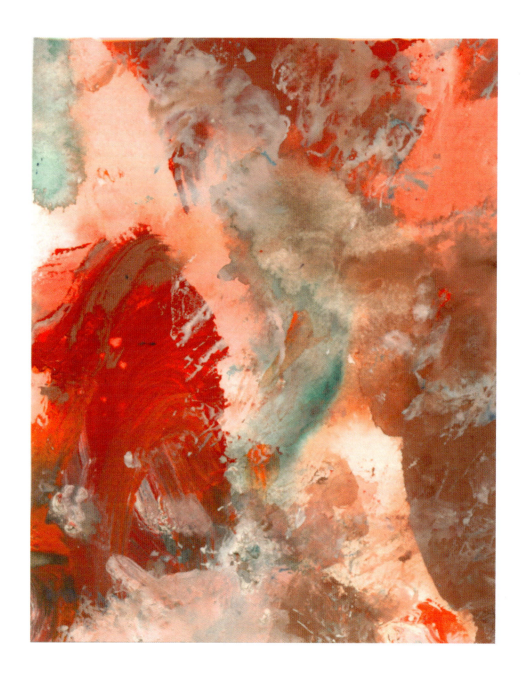

Opposite: After the Rain, watercolor on paper
Tears, watercolor on paper

Galaxy, watercolor on paper
Opposite: Rhapsody, watercolor on paper

Opposite: Joy, watercolor on paper
The Dance, watercolor on paper

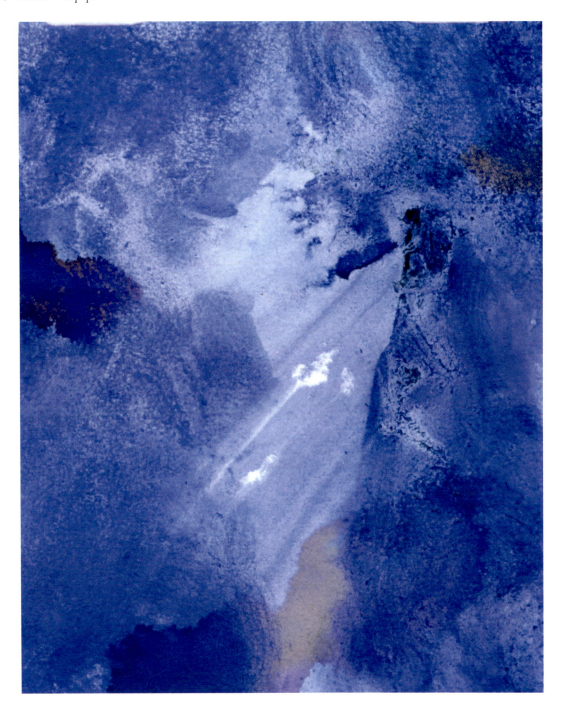

Pandemic Series No. 1, watercolor on paper
Opposite: Pandemic Series No. 2, watercolor on paper

pandemic series

During the COVID pandemic and subsequent lockdowns in 2020 through to 2021, Judy attended art classes online via Zoom. Forced to stay at home, she worked on the *Pandemic Series*. Her palette became darker, and she used salt to create texture. There is a clear contrast between her earlier brighter works and these paintings.

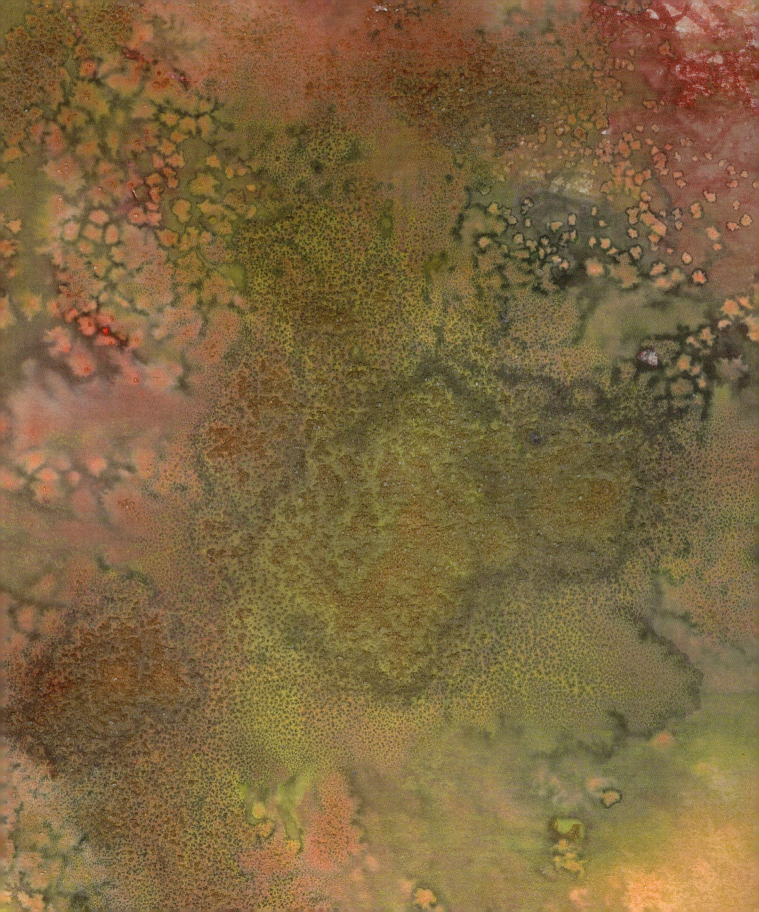

Opposite: Pandemic Series No. 3, watercolor on paper
Pandemic Series No. 4, watercolor on paper

Pandemic Series No. 5, watercolor on paper
Opposite: Pandemic Series No. 6, watercolor on paper

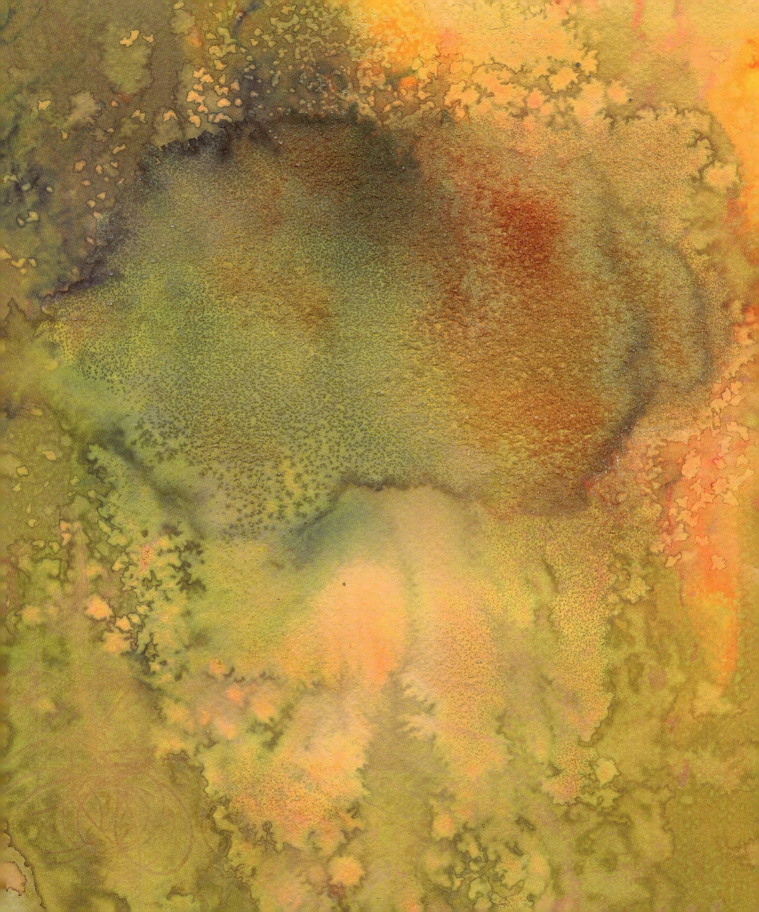

Opposite: Pandemic Series No. 7, watercolor on paper
Pandemic Series No. 8, watercolor on paper

You only appreciate what you have when you don't have it anymore.
Don't take your physical and mental abilities for granted. They
are gifts to be cherished. You can't help the way you were made.
But you can help what you do with what you are.

Judy

Garden, watercolor on paper

list of paintings

Peace, watercolor on paper

Margaret Kay Dodd is an award-winning graphic designer, editor, publisher, and photographer. Born in Australia, she moved to the United States of America via Singapore, and has also lived in Kenya and England. After working in New York City with Simon & Schuster, Inc., Charles Scribner's Sons, and other publishers, she founded Yellow Dog Graphic Works in Santa Barbara, California with Reg van Cuylenburg, followed by Studio K Arts. She has designed and produced many books and fine art catalogs for museums, galleries, and artists. She lives in both Santa Barbara and Den Haag, The Netherlands.